Disney

# Hannah Montana™

## SECRETS AND SUPER SNEAKS

CONTENTS

# WHO'S WHO

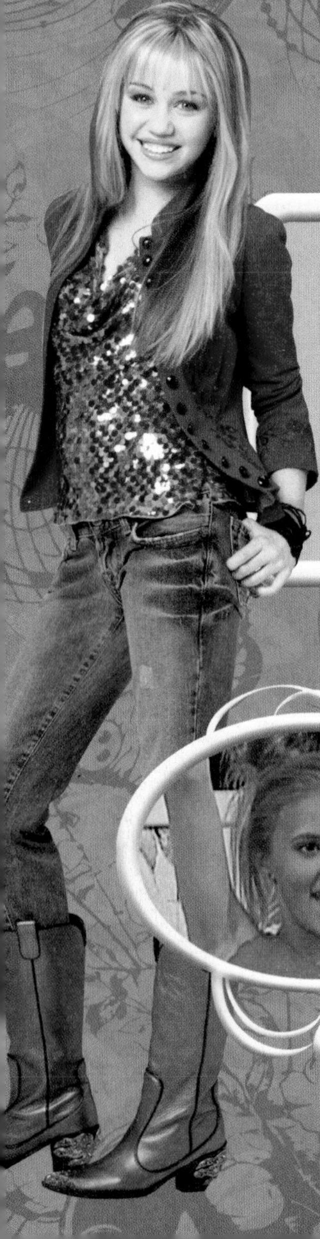

## HANNAH MONTANA/ MILEY

She's the girl next door who just so happens to moonlight as a world-famous pop sensation. But underneath the glamour of a superstar, Miley Stewart is a regular girl who gets into all kinds of sticky situations.

## LILLY

Fun, spontaneous, and just a little bit wacky, Lilly is Miley's best friend and number one partner in crime.

## OLIVER

A super-cool goofball, Oliver is a good friend of both Miley and Lilly.

## ROBBY

Miley's dad is a country musician who knows enough about showbiz to keep his little girl, the pop star, rock solid.

## JACKSON

More silly than slick, Miley's brother Jackson definitely has his own way of doing things.

"LILLY, DO YOU WANT TO KNOW A SECRET?"

# SECRET CELEBRI

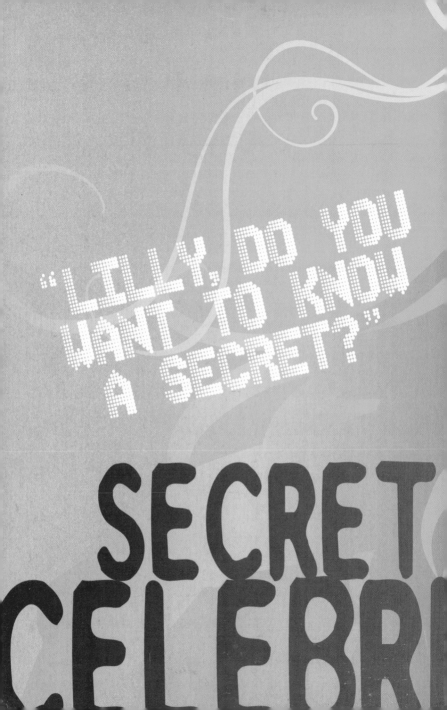

FROM HANNAH'S LATEST MUSIC VIDEO...

In MILEY'S KITCHEn...
BREAKING NEWS!
Fourteen-year-old sensation Hannah Montana continues to ride the wave. Her debut album just went platinum and her sold-out tour continues tomorrow night in Los Angeles.
Hear that, superstar? Hannah Montana: Sold out in Los Angeles.

ugh!
Do you mind? I'm on the phone here.
I have a life, too.
And I would appreciate it if I could have one conversation where I don't have to hear the words *Hannah Montana.*
That's right, babe, I have two incredible seats to Hannah Montana tomorrow night...

Great. See you then.
I need two incredible seats for tomorrow night.
Sorry, I'm sold out.
Dad!
Think about it this way, Miley. He goes out with the girl, they fall in love, they get married, he moves out.

You got the tickets.
RING RING
Hello?
Landing in twenty seconds.
Great!
Lilly in eighteen seconds!
yank!
She's your best friend, Miley. Sooner or later you're gonna have to tell her you're Hannah Montana.
I pick later!

LILLY SAILS IN AIRBORNE ON HER SKATEBOARD...
SWOOSH!
Ahhh... Guess who just landed two tickets to the hottest concert in town?
Miley. You and I—I being your best friend—are going to see the one, the only, Hannah Montana!
Gulp!
You're not screaming. Why aren't you screaming?
Oh believe me, she's screaming on the inside.

SEAVIEW MIDDLE SCHOOL
THE NEXT DAY AT SCHOOL...
I just don't get it. Why won't you go to the concert with me?
It's just that...um, I really want to spend some quality time with my brother.
Quality time with your brother?
Okay, if you don't want to tell me, I guess there's nothing I can do... Except go through life wondering what I did to deserve being hurt so badly by my bestest friend.
Oh, stop, I just can't go, okay? STOP!

THEN JOHNNY, HANNAH'S CRUSH, APPROACHES AND ASKS...
Hey, Miley. How's it going?
Pretty good just getting some ketchup for my veggie burger I see you like mayonnaise I've never tried that on a veggie burger and maybe I should but not today because I've already got the ketchup going and—
Miley, Miley.
squirt!!
You know, what a lot of people don't know is: it's also a wonderful moisturizer.
Here. Isn't that lovely?
Huh, my hand does feel softer.

Wow.
I know. He is so hot. And I am so lame.
Hey! He's the one who believed ketchup was a moisturizer.
Miley, you've been totally crushing on Johnny Collins for months. thought you were funny. is your chance. He's sittin right there. Let's move.
I just can't do it.
Yes, you can. Miley, you're smart, you're funny, and you're totally cute. And now... you have my lucky bracelet.
Okay.

Wait. Booger check.

Oh, you're so gross.

All clear. Good to go.

MILEY AND LILLY HEAD FOR THE SEATS RIGHT NEXT TO JOHNNY.

AMBER AND ASHLEY SLIP INTO MILEY AND LILLY'S SEATS.

Hey, Amber, Ashley. We were going to sit there.

AMBER AND ASHLEY TELL MILEY AND LILLY TO SIT BY THE TRASH CANS AT THE LOSERS' TABLE!

Hey Amber, I think it might be time to pluck the 'stache.
And Ashley, is that a zit or are you growing a new head?
Gross!
Oooh!

SIZZLE!

Okay, we didn't get those seats. Minor setback. But the good news is... we have better seats for Hannah Montana! But I'm not gonna beg. Please!

I'm sorry, I...just don't like Hannah Montana.

What?

OLIVER ENTERS THE CAFETERIA...
Hey, baby. How are you doing?

Oliver, you're not going to believe this. Miley says she doesn't like Hannah Montana.
What? Hannah Montana is a goddess. I worship at her feet. In fact, F.Y.I., someday I'm going to be Mr. Hannah Montana.
Oliver, I say this 'cause I care about you: get some help.
Miley, if you don't take this ticket, I'm going to end up going to the concert with "Mr. Hannah Montana!"
YOU HAVE AN EXTRA TICKET TO HANNAH MONTANA?!!
That was really loud, wasn't it?
Swarm!
Mob!

Hey, Dad. I'm really nervous about my date, and—well, I'm just gonna say this...
...there is nobody in the world whose advice I trust and respect more than you.
Son, I'm not loaning you money.
What? Is that what you think this is about? Dad, I am hurt. This has nothing to do with borrowing money from you.
I was actually kind of hoping for an outright gift.
I gave you the gift of life, son. Don't push it.

Honey, what happened?
Hannah Montana happened.
You mean the kids at school found out?
No, this was just about a ticket to see Hannah Montana. What if they found out I was Hanna
Montana? No one would treat me the same.
I bet Lilly would.
Are you kidding? She's Hannah's biggest fan. If she knew the truth, I'd never be just Miley again.

She's still your best bud and you need to trust that. At least think about telling her.
Okay.
Not gonna happen.
Dad, I only hope that when I'm a father I can give my children–
No money.
Didn't think so.

AT THE HANNAH MONTANA CONCERT...
CHEER!
Hannah Montana...
There you go...
Hi, Joh–ust another fan.
MILEY'S CRUSH
Could you sign it "to Johnny"? It's not me, it's my little brother.
There you go. Really soft hands.
Thanks, it's ketchup.

I hate wearing this thing. It's like kissing your great Aunt Clara.
BLAAH!
SHIVER
Great show tonight.
Your mom would have been so proud of you.
Thanks, Dad.

CREAK
Higher, Oliver. I'm almost in.
There is no higher. You're already standing on my head!
ugh!
Not good.
She sticks the landing!

Wow! Hannah Montana's hot dog!
Hannah Montana's scarf!
Hannah Montana's... Hannah Montana!
AAAAH!
Whoever you are, get out of here right now or I'll call security!
Wait, wait! I'm sorry, I was just looking for a souvenir.
My name's Lilly Truscott and I'm a huge fan.

HMMM...
Ugh!
Did you just shove a pie in your face?
It's not a real pie. It's a... foaming facial wash...pie.
I just wish Miley were here.
Miley? Who's Miley? That's a strange name.
She's my best friend.

Great. Well, why don't you go get her?
Great idea! I'll call her!
RING!
Aren't you gonna get that?
I'm talking to you. That would be rude.
Okay...
RING RING
She's not home.
Wow, that's weird.
SILENCE

Why don't I just give you an autograph for her?
What about me? I'm the one who loves you!
I've really got to go.
Wait, can't I even shampoo your beautiful blonde hair?
No, but you can take this towel.
Hannah Montana's towel!
Ahhhhhh...

Well, I guess I'm leaving, too...
Okay.
With nothing but my memories, which will fade too quickly–
All right, all right. Here.
Oh, my gosh! The actual scarf you wore on the actual stage.
I can't believe it. This is so— Hey, I have a lucky bracelet just like that.

I loaned it to my best friend yesterday.
Of course mine says—
—LILLY.
Just like that.
WIPE
Ta-da!
GASP!

Lilly, I know you're upset I didn't tell you, but you can't just freeze me out like this.
Please talk to me.
I thought we were friends. I thought we told each other everything!
But I guess I was wrong since you kept just about the biggest secret in the world...
...Miley Stewart-slash-Hannah Montana!
Okay...well, other than that, did you enjoy the concert?

Hey, Hannah. I thought my lady here could use a little souvenir.
Jackson, get out of here!
I am so out of here.
Lilly, please wait.
I wanted to tell you, it's just that...I was afraid.
Afraid of what?

I don't know, I thought maybe once you knew you wouldn't want to be my friend anymore and...
...you'd like Hannah Montana more than you like me.
That's what you thought? That could never happen, Miley.
Don't you know that?
Yeah, I do.
Okay, no more secrets. And to prove it, I'm going to show you something I've never shown to any other friend.

BACK AT MILEY'S HOUSE...
Wait until you see this!
Why am I standing in your closet?
Because behind my closet is...
...my closet!
AAAH!
Spin

It's like a dream. A beautiful, beautiful dream.
Okay, dream's over. I've got to have these.
Wait, there's more.
VOILA!
What size do you wear?
I'm five.
I'm six, but I'll squeeze! Wait until Amber and Ashley find out.

No! No one else can see this stuff. Once people know I'm Hannah, they won't treat me the same.
That's the point! I'm talking mega-popularity here.
No!
How can you be so selfish? C'mon, cut me some slack, Hannah.
Hannah?!
Did I say Hannah? I didn't mean that. It was a mistake.
No, the mistake was trusting you.

DASH!
I think things are gonna be a whole lot better around here now that you know our little secret.
Did you see the way she ignored you? I'm sorry, but that is no way to treat a man of your compassion, sensitivity, and–
Still no money?
squirt!!
I am so mad.
Everything I was afraid would happen happened. She found out who I was, and now it's ruined everything.
You don't know that for sure, Miles. Things could change. Just give it some time.
Group hug.
Gotta go.
Outta here.

THE NEXT DAY...
TURN!
I don't know. I think it makes me look a little big around the hips.
Hey, guys. Sorry we're late. Whoa, doggies!
Fermine needed to work on the dress, and he said he'd pay me.
Next time, try something with sleeves, and deodorant.
This is what you get.
Okay, Fermine, what do I owe you?

Daddy! You made him do that?
Hey, the boy said he needed some money. I thought I might as well get a chuckle out of it.
Lilly alert!
Hey, can I talk to you?
Who? Miley or Hannah?
I'm sorry I called you Hannah, but that was major news. You gotta give me a little time to get used to it.
What happens if you can't? What about the next time you get dissed by Amber and Ashley?

Are you sure you won't want to tell them?
Of course I'll *want* to. But I won't. And you know why?
Because you're my best friend. When I was sitting in my room, all upset, you're the one I wanted to talk to, not Hannah Montana.
Well...I guess I've said everything. So...see ya.
Here I go...heading for the door...Still hoping she forgives me...halfway there.
You are such a drama queen. Hugs?
SQUEEZE!

THE NEXT DAY...
See this towel? Hannah gave it to me in her dressing room. She really did.
You're pathetic.
He's telling the truth. And she gave Lilly something, too.
What are you doing?
You'll see.
HEY, EVERYBODY! IT'S HANNAH MONTANA'S SCARF!
AAAAH!
THE END!

Secret
Star

"SHE'S A SUPER SNEAK"

Look at the size of this bad boy. He put up quite a battle too—it was him, then it was me, then it was him, then it was me—
Dad, you got him at the fish mart.
Yeah, but you should've seen the size of the lady that tried to take him from me. It was her, then it was me, then it was—
All right, all right, Dad, I get it.
So what's it gonna be, Bucky, pan-fried or barbecued?
Dad, remember what we said about namin' the fish?

What?
It makes them a little harder to eat.
Dad, I know I have midterms Monday, but the new Ashton Kutcher movie is previewing tonight.
How many "prettys" do I have to put before "please" for you to let me go?
Mile...
Pretty-pretty-pretty-pretty-pretty-pretty–pretty-pretty-pretty-pretty-pretty-please, Dad, please.

Whoa!
I can go?
No, you can stop. You know you gotta study...
Yes, Dad, but if you think about it, midterms are halfway to finals so I only need to study about as half as hard.
And since I already study twice as hard as everybody else, I only need to study a quarter. So I'm done. See how that works?
No, and you know what? I'm the dad. And you lose. See how that works?

You see, little sister: Dad, as a single parent, is just trying to make sure that you have the proper guidance.
And I, for one, commend him on his commitment to education.
Son, I'm glad you see it that way. Because I'm committing you to staying home and studying this weekend, too.
Ha. Ha.
But my midterms were last week!
Yeah, no kidding. I had to wrap the fish in something. See?
Minus!

THAT NIGHT...

I know, Dad, but what I'm sayin' is, who really needs history? It's so...yesterday. And I'm about the future!

Yeah, and so am I. And right now I see you at 35, living with me, no job, still stealing my change off the counter.

This is a book. Go forth and learn.

Remember my "ha, ha" from before? I now add one more "ha," making it a full..."ha, ha..." Wait for it...

Ha!

Now Dad, I know you already said no but I've been studying a lot since then. I sneezed a while ago and algebra came out.

Well next time, sneeze a little smart on your brother. He could use all the help he can get.
I'm heading out for my meeting. I should be back around eleven. I'll be on my cell if anybody needs me—so try not to need me.
I don't know. You guys think I'm being too tough on ya?
Yes.
Good. Then that means I'm doing my job right. Study hard now.
Sigh.

JUGGLE

Yawn!

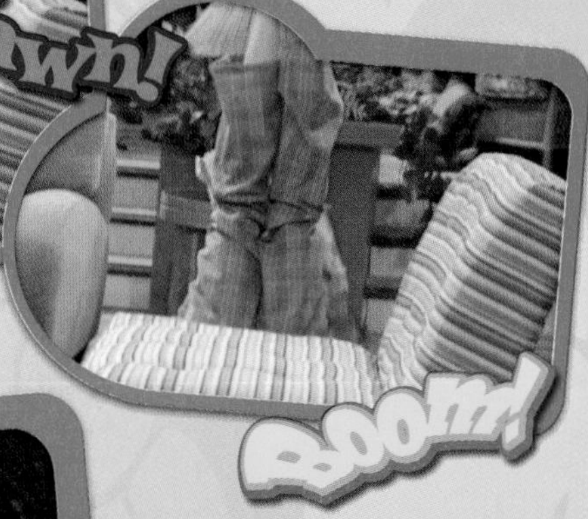
Boom!

Wow. Eight minutes already.
Yup. Time to turn in. Good thing I'm not an outtie.
DING-DONG!
Cover him up...we've got company.
Aw, she don't like me.
So what's the deal? Your dad say yes or no?
Yeah, let's get those feet movin'! My mom's in the car "groovin' to the oldies" and it's getting uglier by the decade.

Lilly, my dad said no.
You think he said no, he really said go. No, go, it's a mistake anybody could make. Come on.
I just can't go.
I heard Ashton Kutcher's gonna be there.
Okay, now you're just being cruel. But that's good, it's workin', keep goin'.
Do it, do it... Ashton...do it...
Uh...just one more time.

Do it.
Okay!
Okay, now all we gotta do is sneak you out without Jackson knowing.
Chug! Chug! Chug! Chug!
He'll never notice. He's got a friend over.
Gotcha.
whisper

Okay, well, gotta go.
Well, I'm just gonna go upstairs and study.
Well, I'm just gonna stay down here and not care.
RING!
RING!
Oh yeah, big dawg. What's up, Cooper?
You gotta get down here.

Theater three? I'm guessing it's very close to theater two. Can't you see I'm on the phone?
I swear, people get dumber and dumber every day.
Hello! You're costing me minutes here!
And I'm telling you this on the D.L.

There is a very hot rumor that Mr. Ashton Kutcher is dropping by here tonight.
And I should care about this because?
Because, this place is gonna be crawling with fine ladies trying to get next to Ashton. And when they can't find him...
... they'll settle for us! Oh yeah!
I don't know, Coop. I mean, if I split, Miley's just gonna tell my Dad...
Of course she is in her room for the rest of the night.

SWOOSH!
And she's such a goody-goody, little Miss Perfect. Always kissing up to Dad.
Just once in her life you'd think she'd go out on a limb or something.
But will she? Unh, unh. Because she is gutless.
NA NA NA NA NA!
You know what? She won't even know that I'm gone. I just talked me into it!

AT THE CINEPLEX...
Cooper, you are a genius. It's like cheerleader tryouts.
Right. Except we don't have to wear those itchy man-sweaters or do the splits. You know, I still can't ride a bike.
POINT
Ah, the things we do for love.
Oh yeah.
Now. How to proceed is the question.

Watch and learn.
Hey, Ashton! Mister Kutcher! My man!
The Kutchinator! Kutchy kutchy you!
What's that, my close personal friend? Come to your party tonight? Sure. I'll just find myself a little hottie, and we'll party like it's 19–
RING!
RING!
RING!

Hello? Hey, Barry. Can I maybe give you a call back?
GROAN!

Ladies!
Very smooth. You know I was watching and learning and what I learned was I should not have watched.

All right, have a little patience, my man. It's just a minor setback.

Prepare to be impressed.

So... Mr. Kutcher! The Kutchking! Volcanic Ash!

Aaaaaahh!...
TWIRL
What are you doing here?
Me?! What about you?!
I'm telling Dad!
No, you're not.

Because we're not really here right now.
Right. But Dad is!
HIDE!
What can I say, Dad? She snuck out, I followed her here, I'm just as disappointed as you are.

What are you doing?
What does it look like I'm doing? I'm gettin' ready to sell you out.
Listen, buster, if I go down, I'm taking you with me! What's he doing here? He said he had a meeting.
All right, just calm down. All we have to do is wait 'til he goes in, he'll never know you were here.
Lilly? Miley?
grab!
PST!

Miley's dad's here.
Great!
He doesn't know we're here. And we're gonna try to keep it that way.
Crash!
AAAAH!
I don't think we're off to a good start.

grab!

the MYSTERY

EEK!!

We have gotta get out of here!
USING THE CARDBOARD CUTOUT AS A SHIELD, THEY HEAD FOR THE EXIT.
Wait, my bag!
Halt!
REACH!
OOPS!

grab!
Peek!
DIAL...
Don't answer it. Keep moving!
RiNG!
I have to answer it. He thinks we're at home.
Hey, Dad! We're home!
Studying at home.
Where we are. Home.

Yeah, I just called to check in on you guys and let you know...
...that whatever it is that you're doing that you don't want me to know you're doing, stop doing it.
Study hard now. Bye.
I hate lying to him.
You're on your hands and knees in a movie theater! The honesty ship has sailed.
I just can't figure one thing out: Why are we hiding?
Oh, Oliver, you naive, simple boy... with a very good point!
Best of luck!
DASH!

Perfect. Could this night get any worse?
Depends on how you feel about that.
I don't believe it.
I know. The old man can get a date and I can't!

BACK AT HOME...
Why would Dad do this? Why did he go on a date and not tell us?
I don't know.
Please stop stuffing your face?
I'm eating away the pain.
Doesn't this bother you?
Miley, it's been three years. He's probably lonely.
Well, then we'll get him a puppy!

I hear him!
Look, just remember that whatever happens, he can't know we were there. So just play it cool.
I will. I will. He won't suspect a thing.
Where have you been? We agreed you'd be home by eleven. And it's...
Eleven oh three?
Exactly! Three minutes of pure agony!

Yes, but the important thing is that, while you were out, we weren't.
Right. And you were at, um, a meetin How did that go?
Fine.
Fine? One syllable? That's all I get?
Okay, it was really fine. Three syllables. Keep the change.
Daddy, you're always talking about how we don't share enough and you're right.
We should. Starting now. You go first.

Okay. It was a very... productive meeting and who knows, in time it could amount to a little som'n-som'n...
Like what-what?
I don't know. You know how if you talk about things too early, it might jinx it?
But don't worry, if it keeps going the way it's going, I'll tell you all about it.
Love you guys. Good night.
Love you, too.
Good night, Dad.
Well, great. This is terrible. He's happy!

THE NEXT MORNING...
I just wish I knew something about this woman. What does she do for a living? Does she have any kids?
Any dogs? A sound-proof basement where no one can hear our screams? I don't even know her name.
Margo Diamond.
What?
Dad's Palm Pilot. Movie Saturday night... Margo Diamond.
Hey, isn't she that real estate lady, you know, the one on the bus bench in front of the library?

Your dad's dating a homeless real estate lady?
Wow, that's weird, she sells houses, but doesn't have one.
I meant the ad on the bench, Mrs. Einstein.
This is perfect. Now you can go meet her. Jackson can drive you.
Let me paint you guys a little picture here.
Hi, I'm Miley Stewart...
...and I'm her brother Jackson.

And we snuck out to the movies last night and saw that you were on a date with our father.
Now why are we telling you this?
Out of some insane desire to wanna get caught and be grounded for the rest of our natural lives!
Okay, how com you always get t be the apple?
Wait a minute. Belly Button Boy makes sense.
Okay, maybe you are right. Maybe we can't go down there and talk to her.
But I know someone who can.

AT THE REALTOR'S OFFICE...
This is the dumbest thing I've ever done for you.
This is the only thing you've ever done for me.
And don't pretend you're not the least bit interested in our future possible stepmom.
Well, of course I am. You're not the only one who cares about Dad. I want him to be happy, too.
And if she happens to have a hot daughter who likes to invite her friends over for pillow fights, well, everybody wins!
Hello! Back to earth, Captain Hormone. All right, let's do this.
Just remember you're my chauffeur.

Um. Hi. I'm Hannah Montana, and I'm looking for a house.
That is the stupidest thing I've ever heard!
Lady, you're not gonna sell many houses with that attitude.
Sorry. Telephone.
Hi. Ah, what a thrill to meet you. My niece is a big fan of yours.
Really? Well, how old is she? What does she look like and do you happen to have a picture of her?
Not why we're here.

But if we are going to be in business together, I do need to know a little about you first.
For example, who's this?
Your husband?! Does he know you're dating?
Wait a minute. That's my brother.
A likely story. Who keeps a picture of their brother on their desk?
He gave me a kidney.
So you're scarred.

You know, that's getting a little personal. Can we just stick to houses?
Certainly.
What's yours like? Um, any kids running around?
Ah, daughters who like pillow fights?
WHAT?
You know, uh, you know, maybe I am not the right person to be selling you a house.

TAP!
TAP!
TAP!
Let me put you in touch with Habib, Prince of the West Side. You're gonna love him.
GASP!
Hey, I'm not finished yet. On second thought, yes I am.
POINT!
Ms. Diamond, excuse me and my chauffeur...we have to confer...in private.
And I must insist that you let no one know that I was here!
CRAWL

Ah, I don't know what to say, Dad.

It was her idea. I tried to stop her. I'm just as disappointed as you are.

I am amazed that you can stand without a spine.

Hi. I brought you these.

Jackson, you're on my foot!
I can't move. I've got a For Sale sign...in my backyard.
I had a nice time last night.
Man, he really likes her.
You know, Miles, she does seem pretty nice.
I don't care how nice she is, she ain't ever gettin' any of my kidneys!

MARGO TELLS ROBBY SHE'D LOVE TO GO OUT FOR COFFEE, BUT THAT SHE NEEDS TO GET SOMEONE TO COVER FOR HER. BEFORE SHE LEAVES TO GET HER COAT, MARGO TELLS HIM SHE'S GOT HANNAH MONTANA HIDING IN HER CLOSET...

Would it help if I said I was happy for you?
How could you?
Whoa, now hold up, little girl. How'd you find out?
Well, *you* didn't tell me.

I can explain.
Okay, explain this: why are you dating someone without telling me?
Explain how you could ever think that there's someone out there...
...who could ever replace my mom?
That was awkward.
SIGH!

BACK AT HOME...
That's a beautiful song, honey.
I like coming out here at night. It's a good place to try and figure things out.
Maybe we could figure out things together.
Why didn't you tell me?
I guess I was hoping to tell you at just the right time and just the right way...
But I guess there was no right time, was there?

I just can't picture you with anybody else but Mom.
Neither can I. What she and I had was special. I can't replace that.
Then why are you dating?
Because life goes on. And we gotta try and figure out some way to go on with it.
Don't you think your mom would've wanted that for us?
Yeah, I guess she would've. She was pretty smart that way...I really miss her, Daddy.
I miss her too, kiddo.

HUH?
What's this rope ladder doing there?
Uh, Dad, let's not ruin the beautiful moment.
You're right.
I'll ruin it tomorrow.
HUG

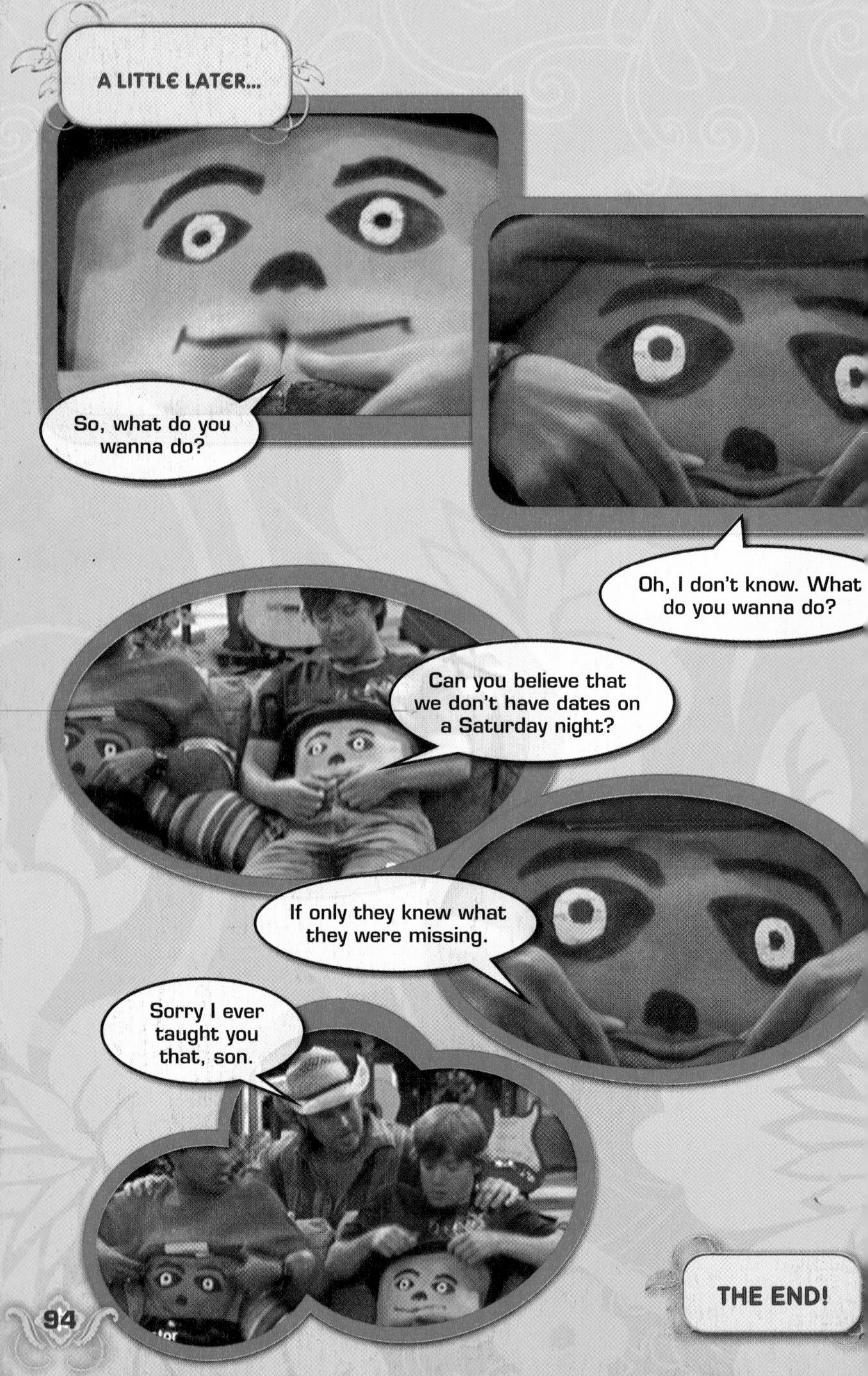
A LITTLE LATER...
So, what do you wanna do?
Oh, I don't know. What do you wanna do?
Can you believe that we don't have dates on a Saturday night?
If only they knew what they were missing.
Sorry I ever taught you that, son.
THE END!

Best friends...
...forever!

As long as I have my friends by my side, I'm happy.

Disney
Hannah Montana
TOKYOPOP
Hamburg · London · Los Angeles · Tokyo

Julie Taylor
ng Editor - Marion Brown
signer and Letterer - Anna Kernbaum
over Designer - Monalisa J. de Asis
Graphic Artist - Monalisa J. de Asis

Production Manager - Elisabeth Brizzi
Art Director - Anne Marie Horne
VP of Production - Ron Klamert
Editor in Chief - Rob Tokar
Publisher - Mike Kiley
President & C.O.O. - John Parker
C.E.O. & Chief Creative Officer - Stuart Levy

E-mail: info@TOKYOPOP.com
Come visit us online at www.TOKYOPOP.com

A TOKYOPOP® Cine-Manga® Book
TOKYOPOP Inc.
5900 Wilshire Blvd., Suite 2000
Los Angeles, CA 90036

Hannah Montana Volume 1


ISBN: 978-1-4278-0281-1



First TOKYOPOP® printing: July 2007

10 9 8 7 6 5 4 3 2 1

Printed in the USA

3/0

# HANN
# MONTAN



Based on the television series, "Hannah Montana,"
Created By
Michael Poryes and Rich Correll & Barry O'Brien

# SECRETS AND SUPER SNEAKS

## "Lilly, Do You Want to Know a Secret?"

Written By Steven Peterman, Gary Dontzig and Michael Poryes

## "She's a Super Sneak"

Written By Kim Friese